DITCH the CARBS

LOW CARB
– starter pack –

sugar free • grain free • gluten free

25 easy recipes

The Complete Beginners' Guide
Sample menu | Shopping lists | Progress tracker

Libby Jenkinson

LOW CARB STARTER PACK

Libby Jenkinson

Follow via

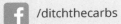 /ditchthecarbs

/+Ditchthecarbs

ditchthecarbs

ditchthecarbs

 easylowcarbrecipes.tumblr.com

 ditchthe_carbs

 Ditch The Carbs

SUBSCRIBE

 www.ditchthecarbs.com/subscribe-now

Welcome to
"Low Carb Starter Pack"

I will show you the basic recipes you need for the best possible start to low-carb living.

Welcome and congratulations! You have taken the first step to living sugar free and low carb.

I will show you how to give up sugar, how to start eating low carb and what to cook. I will show you how to give up processed food and start eating real whole food.

My easy-to-follow guide is perfect for beginners. There are recipes, shopping lists, a sample meal plan and printables to get you started.

All these recipes are my go-to meals and excellent choices for beginners. My recipes are all sugar free, grain free, gluten free and low carb. I use basic ingredients and nothing that is difficult to find.

I have included breakfasts, lunches, dinners, snacks and sweet treats. I will show you how to start cooking the low-carb and sugar-free way.

Let's get started.

Libby Jenkinson

Founder at ditchthecarbs.com

Contents

Recipes

NO sugars grains
Only healthy fats

SUGAR FREE

■ Why sugar free?

Sugar raises insulin which is our fat-storing hormone. Insulin drives body fat and drives hunger.

Our bodies are not designed to eat as much sugar as we do. Sugar used to be a scarce commodity but is now found in 80% of processed food. By the time a child reaches eight years old, they have consumed as much sugar as an adult would have consumed in their entire life a century ago.

Sugar is far more harmful than just being empty calories. Sugar and processed food crowds out nutrition. Sugar drives insulin, appetite and fat storage. The constant high levels of sugar and insulin in our body is damaging. High levels of insulin eventually lead to insulin resistance and inflammation which are the root cause of many modern diseases. Sugar is the main cause of tooth decay, obesity, type 2 diabetes , increased risk of heart disease, some cancers, and dementia.

Have you ever wondered why you are constantly eating yet constantly hungry? Sugar. Sugar and your insulin response control your appetite and weight gain. Remove sugar from your diet and you will be in control of your appetite and weight. Skin will improve and concentration will be clearer.

Eating low carb reduces inflammation and reduces the risk of developing the Big 4 – obesity, type 2 diabetes, cancer and heart disease.

■ Why go low carb?

"Carbohydrates are glucose molecules stuck together"

Important ::

This is LOW CARB not NO CARB.
Low-carb eating focuses on reducing how much of our daily diet comes from unnecessary processed carbohydrates. It is a way of eating that keeps us fuller for longer and improves our nutrition beyond all belief. We eat low-carb, real, whole food and plenty of healthy fats.

All carbohydrates are converted into sugar in the body. It doesn't matter whether it's table sugar, organic coconut sugar, wholegrain bread, pasta, oats, rice or potatoes, they all raise our blood sugar which causes a release of insulin. Each person has a different tolerance to carbohydrate in their diet and everyone has a different insulin sensitivity.

Children who are active and within a healthy weight range can tolerate more carbs and are more insulin sensitive than a middle-aged person, a sedentary person or an overweight person. Those with diabetes (type 1 and type 2) are intolerant to carbs so restricting their carbs will improve blood-sugar control and reduce the risk of diabetic complications.

Low carb is the most wonderful, nutritious, healthy, natural and colourful way to eat. Our meals are no longer filled with beige carbs such as pasta, rice, processed bread, high-sugar sweets or liquid sugar such as juice and sodas. They will be filled with colour, variety and vibrancy. Once you understand how processed carbohydrates such as pasta and bread have been crowding out the nutrition in your meals, you will understand what a wonderful fresh way of eating this is.

Think of an average meal such as a sandwich or spaghetti bolognese. The nutritious part is the filling, salad, meat or sauce and cheese, yet the bulk of the meal is made up from cheap processed carbohydrates in the form of bread or pasta. Take those carbs away and we are left with the nutritious part of the meal which we should be eating more of.

So base your meals on real low-carb foods that are high in nutrition, vitamins, minerals, antioxidants, and phytonutrients. Base your meals on non-starchy vegetables, dairy, nuts, seeds, low-sugar fruit and meat. Real, whole food.

■ Why grain free?

GRAIN FREE

The grains that are found in almost all processed foods these days are completely different to the grains our ancestors were raised on.

Grains have been modified to be shorter (easier to harvest), more disease resistant and higher in starch. Grains are grown, sprayed and processed altogether differently to ancient methods. Insecticides used on crops are affecting the health of our gut, immunity, and ever-more common allergies.

Never in the history of mankind have grains appeared at every single meal and snack. Modern processing and farming have left grains so devoid of nutrition that cereals and breads have to be fortified.

Grains have been used for centuries to fatten animals before slaughter, and geese are force fed grains to make foie gras (fatty liver pate).

Cereals are now resembling desserts rather than a hearty breakfast. Breakfast cereals are made with cheap grains, fortified, with added flavours, preservatives and sugar. Their excessive sugar can easily exceed our daily sugar limit.

"Simply by cutting out sugar and grains, we eliminate most of the processed foods. By eating real whole food and cooking from scratch, we become low carb almost by default."

■ What is a healthy fat?

Saturated fats and monounsaturated fats are stable and less likely to become oxidised. Oils such as olive oil, coconut oil, macadamia oil and avocado oil are simple, pressed oils. Butter and lard and naturally occurring from animals. Healthy fats are those higher in omega 3 (anti-inflammatory) and lower in omega 6 (inflammatory). A naturally occurring healthy fat is as close to nature intended it and requires as little processing as possible.

Vegetable oils such as canola oil, rice bran oil, soybean oil, sunflower oil, corn oil and margarine are unstable, incredibly processed and easily oxidised. They are high in omega 6 which causes inflammation. Trans fats are the most inflammatory. These unhealthy oils are found in almost all processed foods.

■ Why eat more healthy fat?

There are three macronutrients we eat every day. Carbohydrate, protein and fat. If we decrease the carbs we must increase the healthy fats in our diet. That's not to say it gives us an open invitation to eat fried fatty food, it's about increasing our healthy fats and at the same time reducing our carbs. If we don't reduce our carbs but increase our fats, we are on a high fat and high carb diet, the SAD diet (Standard American Diet). This is the most damaging diet which causes obesity and heart disease.

Including more healthy fats in our diet keeps us fuller for longer. Healthy fats keep us satiated. Healthy fats make our meals tasty and flavoursome. Healthy fats allow us to absorb all the fat-soluble vitamins (A, D, E and K) from a meal.

■ Why avoid low-fat products?

Most low-fat products have had the natural fats stripped away and sugar and chemicals added to improve the taste and texture. Avoid buying low-fat products for both these reasons. Start comparing nutrition labels at the supermarket for low-fat products vs the full-fat version. Lite yoghurts for example can contain 25% sugar compared to natural unsweetened yoghurt which is 4%.

■ How much to eat?

Low carb – Moderate protein – Healthy fats

- **Carbs** – There is no strict definition of low carb but even just lowering your carbs is beneficial. Many regard 50g total carbs per day as a starting point. You may wish to eat more than this when starting, or you may wish to reduce your carb intake further if your weight loss has stalled.

- **Protein** – Aim for 0.6g per lb lean body weight (equivalent to 1–1.5g protein per kg). Too much protein will cause your blood sugar to rise and too little can cause loss of muscle.

- **Fat** – Eat healthy fats until full. Do not overindulge, do not eat to excess, but do not skimp on healthy fats. Eat plenty of healthy fats to keep you full until the next meal and to stop you from snacking.

- **Only eat when hungry.**

■ Health benefits

Many wonderful and amazing health benefits occur when we go low carb and sugar free.

1. Nutrition in improved because we are eating meat, vegetables, healthy fats, nuts, seeds and berries

2. Stable blood sugars and stable appetite

3. Reduced risk of many modern diseases through reducing inflammation

4. Improved our insulin sensitivity

5. Improved mood with stable blood sugars. Achieve a sense of calm

6. Increased energy and concentration, throughout the day

7. Reduced your risk of the Big 4 – obesity, type 2 diabetes, dementia and many cancers

8. Improved skin tone and clarity

"Crowd out junk with nutritious foods"

HOW
to start

"Strive for improvement, not perfection"

There are two options to cut the processed food, sugar and carbs.

1. Go cold turkey – clear out your pantry and start your new way of eating from today.
2. Start slowly – improve as you continue

The option you choose is up to you. You may wish to go cold turkey because having sugar and junk food in the house is too tempting. It can be quite cathartic and cleansing to throw away all your processed junk food and restock your pantry and fridge with real healthy food. However others prefer for it to be a gradual process.

For a family to go low carb and sugar free you may wish to consider starting slowly to avoid arguments and conflict. The transition can be slow, easy, gradual and enjoyable. Considering you may have been eating sweets, cakes, cereals, juices and bread for decades, a few more weeks or months may make the journey an easier and more sustainable one.

■ How to give up sugar & carbs slowly

Use this stepwise approach. Move on to the next step as you feel ready to do so.

1	Stop drinking sugar and carbs – no more juice, fruit smoothies, flavoured coffees, flavoured milks, energy drinks and soda. These are nothing more than liquid sugar. If you really are addicted to these, try these tips. Dilute juice each time until it becomes tasteless, swap soda for diet soda, make your own sugar free flavoured coffees and milk. These measures are temporary because eventually drinking all sugary drinks must stop.
2	Stop eating sweets and confectionery – sweets, ice cream, dried fruit and candy. They're are all sugar bombs. Ignore any claims that some candy or ice cream contains real fruit juice or is organic, it's all sugar – simple. Start buying dark chocolate with the highest % cocoa you can tolerate. The higher the % cocoa, generally the lower the carbs and sugar.
3	Cookies, cakes and pastries – these are high in sugar, grains and carbs, but also unhealthy fats. Start making your own low-carb and sugar-free treats occasionally.
4	Cut back on bread, rice and pasta – aim for one or two bread free lunches each week and one or two pasta/rice free meals. Rice, bread and pasta are purely cheap bulking agents with little or no nutritional value. Make simple swaps such as zoodles instead of spaghetti, enjoy a curry with coconut cauliflower rice, and make a stir fry with no rice, just double or triple the vegetables.

Once you start on this path of eating real, whole, unprocessed food, you won't want to go back. That's the beauty of this way of eating, it's not a short-term diet. It is a lifelong way of eating for lifelong health benefits.

Which sweeteners to use?

Part of the ethos of going low carb is to give up sweet treats apart from special occasions. You may want more sweet low-carb and sugar-free treats when just starting out. As time goes on, you will be relying on these less and less. These are the sweeteners you will often see in sugar-free baking.

Recommended

Stevia or erythritol – Both are natural sweeteners which do not raise blood sugars. Stevia is 300 times sweeter than sugar. Stevia can be bought in the supermarket as concentrated drops or can be bought blended with erythritol so it measures spoon for spoon in place of sugar. It can be easy to oversweeten a recipe using stevia drops. Granules/powder are easier to use. Stevia may give a slight bitter aftertaste if you use too much. Add sweeteners to your taste, because as time goes on, your sweet tooth will diminish and require less.

Not recommended

'Natural' alternatives – Another label for sugar but just in another form. Honey, coconut sugar, molasses, agave, rice malt syrup, dried fruit, Medjool dates – all are forms of sugar. Be suspicious when a recipe says "refined sugar free" because it usually means they have just used another type of sugar.

∎ What is real food?

Real whole food
- has minimal intervention or processing as possible
- is food that your grandmother would recognise
- is fresh and will rot
- close as possible as nature intended it
- are ingredients not products
- is not fake food with colours, preservatives, chemicals, and other nasties
- should not have a long list of hard to pronounce ingredients on the label
- if in doubt, don't buy it

Let's get started

Shopping lists – Printables – Sample menu – Recipes – Tracker

What you can eat

Eat low carb, moderate protein, healthy fats
Eat until full, do not overindulge
Learn to understand appetite vs hunger
Remember: no sugars, no grains, only healthy fats

Vegetables & fruit

- Asparagus
- Aubergine
- Avocados
- Berries
- Bok choy
- Broccoli
- Brussels sprouts
- Cabbage
- Cauliflower
- Celery
- Courgettes
- Cucumber
- Eggplant
- Fennel
- Garlic
- Herbs
- Kale
- Lemons
- Lettuce
- Limes
- Mushrooms
- Onions
- Peppers
- Salad ingredients
- Silver beet
- Spinach
- Spring onions
- Swiss chard
- Tomatoes
- Zucchini

Meat & fish

- Bacon – off the bone (unsweetened)
- Beef – all cuts, mince, ground, steaks
- Chicken – all cuts, skin on, mince, ground, whole
- Crab
- Duck – all cuts, skin on, whole
- Fish – fresh or frozen
- Ham – off the bone (unsweetened)
- Lamb – all cuts, chops, roast, mince, ground, steaks
- Organ meats – liver, kidney etc
- Oysters
- Pepperoni – as unprocessed as possible
- Pork
- Prawns
- Prosciutto
- Salami
- Salmon – fresh or canned in olive oil or brine
- Sardines in oil
- Sausages – more than 85% meat and minimal processing
- Shellfish – mussels, oysters etc
- Shrimp
- Tuna – fresh or canned in olive oil or brine
- Turkey – all cuts

Fridge

- Butter
- Cheese – all types full fat, brie, Camembert, feta, mozzarella, Parmesan,
- Cream – full fat, heavy, double, whipping
- Cream cheese – full fat
- Eggs
- Milk – full fat
- Yoghurt – full fat, unsweetened

Pantry

- Almond meal/flour/ground
- Cocoa unsweetened
- Coconut butter
- Coconut cream (>20% fat)
- Coconut milk (<20% fat)
- Coconut flour
- Coconut unsweetened – shredded, desiccated, threads, chips, fresh
- Chocolate > 80% cocoa
- Gelatin
- Herbs & spices
- Mustard powder
- Nuts – almonds, brazil, hazelnuts, macadamia, pecans, walnuts
- Nut butters
- Olives – green, black, stuffed
- Psyllium husk
- Salsa unsweetened
- Seeds – flaxseeds, linseeds, pumpkin, sunflower,
- Sweetener of choice – stevia or erythritol
- Tahini
- Tea/ coffee
- Vanilla

Freezer

- Berries
- Fish
- Prawns
- Spinach

Healthy fat

- Healthy fats
- Avocado oil
- Butter
- Coconut oil
- Ghee
- Lard
- Macadamia oil
- Olive oil – extra virgin

Kitchen gadgets & equipment

- Food processor
- Spiraliser
- Slow cooker
- Stick blender/immersion blender
- Waffle maker

Remember how far
you have come,
not how far
you have yet to go

– Low Carb –
RECIPES

notes

ditchthecarbs.com

– Low Carb –
Breakfast

- Breakfast McMuggins
- The ultimate LCHF breakfast
- Keto waffles
- Fennel & ginger grain-free granola
- Smoked salmon scrambled eggs

Breakfast McMuggins

Breakfast McMuggins
quick & easy

What could be quicker (and healthier) than a mug cake for breakfast, only this one is savoury and you get to choose exactly the flavours you love. McMuggins are a great way to use leftovers. And don't worry if you don't use a microwave, these can be cooked in the oven in muffin trays.

Quantities per McMuggin

2 tbsp/25g butter

1 tbsp almond flour/meal

2 eggs

1 tbsp spring onion, thinly sliced

2 tbsp grated/shredded cheese

2 tbsp cooked diced meat (bacon, ham, chicken, salami ...)

Salt/pepper to taste

Favourite herbs (I like rosemary)

Leftover veggies

1. Oil or butter a microwaveable heatproof mug or muffin tray.

2. Place the butter in the mug and microwave for 20 seconds or until melted.

3. Stir in the ground almonds.

4. Add all other ingredients and stir together with a fork.

5. Microwave on 'high' for 1 minute, remove and stir with a fork.

6. Microwave on 'high' for a further 1 minute or until cooked in the centre.

7. If you are cooking the McMuggins in an oven, cook at 180C/350F in oiled muffin trays for 10-15 minutes.

Serving size: 1 McMuggin | Calories: 533 | Fat: 48g | Total carbs: 5g
Sugar: 1.8g | Fibre: 1.5g | Protein: 22g

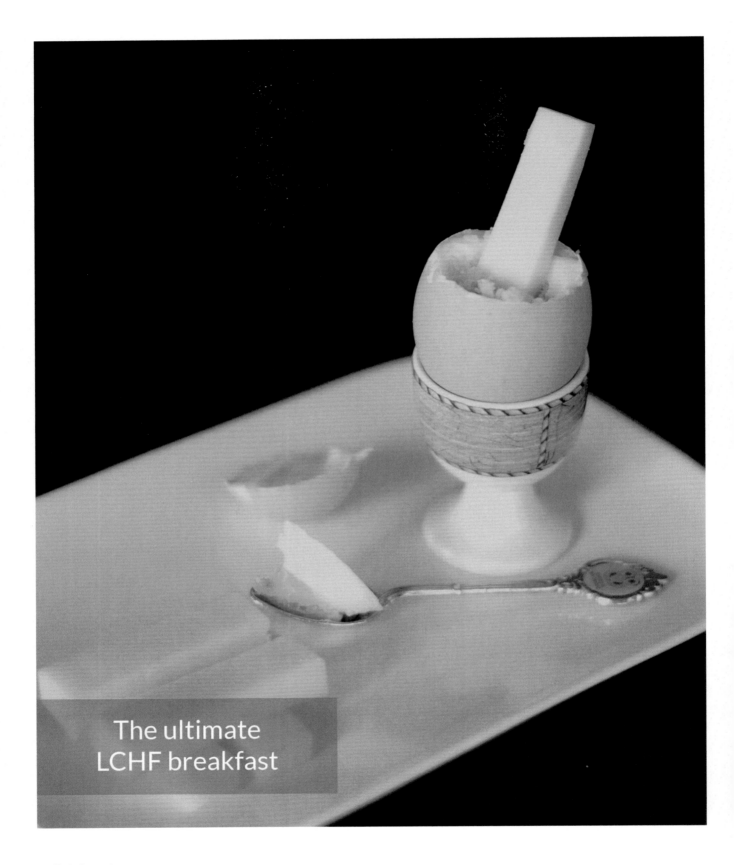

The ultimate
LCHF breakfast

The ultimate LCHF breakfast
boiled eggs with cheese soldiers

You will learn so many different ways to eat eggs for breakfast. They are the most simple and complete meal, whether scrambled, boiled or fried. But how about boiled eggs with cheese soldiers?

Quantities per person

1 egg

50g/1.8 oz full-fat cheese
cut into sticks (soldiers)

1. Place your egg in a saucepan of cold water, cover with a lid and bring the water and eggs to the boil.

2. Once the water is really boiling and bubbling away, turn the heat off, and place the saucepan (with the water and eggs) to rest away from the heat.

3. Set your timer and leave your eggs in the saucepan of hot water for the following times.

   Soft and runny centre = 4 minutes
   Semi-soft centre = 6 minutes
   Medium = 10 minutes

   Once your eggs are cooked to your liking, drain the water immediately and either serve hot or run under cold water to be kept in the fridge once completely cooled

Serving size: 1 egg and cheese soldiers | Calories: 271 | Fat: 21.5g | Total carbs: 1.1g
Sugar: 0.6g | Protein: 17.6g

Keto waffles

Keto waffles
no sugars, no grains

Make a double or triple batch of keto waffles every time. They freeze really well and make great sandwich alternatives.

5 eggs, separated

4 tbsp coconut flour

3-5 tbsp granulated sweetener of choice, to taste

1 tsp baking powder

1–2 tsp vanilla

3 tbsp full-fat milk

125g/4.5 oz butter melted

First bowl.
1. Whisk the egg whites until firm and forming stiff peaks

Second bowl
1. Mix the egg yolks, coconut flour, stevia, and baking powder.

2. Add the melted butter slowly, mixing to ensure it is a smooth consistency.

3. Add the milk and vanilla, mix well.

4. Gently fold spoons of the whisked egg whites into the yolk mixture. Try to keep as much of the air and fluffiness as possible.

5. Place enough of the waffle mixture into the warm waffle maker to make one waffle. Cook until golden.

6. Repeat until all the mixture has been used.

Serving size: 1 waffle (serves 5) | Calories: 280 | Fat: 26g | Total carbs: 4.5g
Sugar: 1.4g | Fibre: 2g | Protein: 7g

Fennel & ginger grain-free granola

Fennel & ginger grain-free granola
a great basic granola recipe

This is my basic grain-free granola recipe. You can adapt the flavours to your liking. I have many more grain-free granolas on the website such as chocolate, cinnamon, or plain. All quantities are approximate and can be changed to what you have in your pantry.

400g/14 oz/4 cups unsweetened shredded/desiccated coconut

150g/5 oz/1 cup sunflower seeds

150g/5 oz/1 cup pumpkin seeds

2 tbsp dried fennel seeds

2 tbsp ground ginger

2 tbsp ground cardamon

4–6 tbsp granulated sweetener of choice, to taste

150g/5 oz/2/3 cup coconut oil, melted

1. Place all the ingredients in a large roasting dish.

2. Mix together with a large spoon.

3. Bake in the oven at 180C/350F for 20 minutes but you must turn the mixture every 3–4 minutes. I set my timer each time I put it back in the oven as it is too darn easy to forget and lose an expensive batch of grain-free granola if it accidentally burns.

4. Once the entire grain-free granola is browned and baked, remove from the oven and allow to cool completely before placing in storage jars.

Serving size: ½ cup/50g/1.8 oz | Calories: 327 | Fat: 32g | Total carbs: 9.5g
Sugar: 2.1g | Fibre: 5.5g | Protein: 6g

Smoked salmon
scrambled eggs

Smoked salmon scrambled eggs
with cream cheese & greens

After all these years of being low carb, I still think this is my favourite recipe for breakfast. It has the most perfect combination of salmon to give us wonderful omega 3, eggs for protein, cream cheese for healthy fats and leafy greens for all that fiber, nutrients and vitamins – not to mention a colour combination a slice of toast can't compete with.

Per person

2 tbsp/28g/1 oz butter

2 cups leafy greens, roughly chopped

2 eggs

2 tbsp/30ml full-fat cream

56g/2 oz smoked salmon

2 tbsp/28g/1 oz full-fat cream cheese

+/- salt and pepper

1. In a frying pan, heat half of the butter. Add the chopped leafy greens, salt and pepper and stir until they are wilted. Remove from the frying pan and place on the serving dish.

2. In a small bowl, whisk the eggs and milk together with a fork. Melt the remaining butter in the hot frying pan, then pour the scrambled egg mixture on top. Stir gently to make fluffy scrambled eggs.

3. Place the warm scrambled eggs on top of the cooked leafy greens, add smoked salmon then garnish with the cream cheese.

Serving size: 1 serve | Calories: 621 | Fat: 55g | Total carbs: 5g
Sugar: 3g | Fibre: 1.3g | Protein: 26g

notes

– Low Carb –
Lunch

- Basic skillet bread
- Crustless salmon quiche
- Caesar salad
- Courgette & feta fritters
- Salmon zoodles

Basic
skillet bread

Basic skillet bread
your go-to bread recipe

A fabulous basic bread recipe to cook in the skillet or frying pan. Add your favourite herbs and spices to make this just the way you like it. Serve warm with butter.

2 tbsp/25g butter for frying

4 eggs

⅓ cup natural unsweetened natural yoghurt

1 ½ tbsp psyllium husk

¾ cup almond meal/flour

1 tsp baking powder

1 tbsp herbs

½ tsp salt

½ cup grated/shredded cheese

¼ cup grated/shredded Parmesan

Bowl 1
1. Whisk the eggs until pale and frothy.
2. Fold in the yoghurt.

Bowl 2
1. Mix all the other dry ingredients.
2. Pour the wet ingredients from bowl 1 into the centre and fold together gently.
3. Let the mixture rest for 5–10 minutes to allow the psyllium husk to absorb the liquid and swell.
4. Heat the butter in the skillet/frying pan on a low/medium heat.
5. Pour the entire mixture into the skillet/frying pan and cook slowly until the surface is no longer wet and small bubbles appear.
6. Flip the skillet bread over and cook until golden on the other side.
7. Flip the skillet bread onto a plate and sprinkle with salt.

Serving size: 1 slice (makes 8 slices) | Calories: 170 | Fat: 14g | Total carbs: 7g
Sugar: 1g | Fibre: 4g | Protein: 8g

Crustless salmon quiche

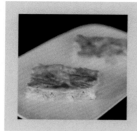

Crustless salmon quiche
simple and light

This is such and easy and economical way to make an expensive piece of salmon stretch for a family. You can also bake the quiche mixture in mini muffin tins ready for school lunches or a snack.

500g/17.6 oz fresh salmon fillet, diced/cubed

8 eggs

250g/8.8 oz cream cheese diced/cubed

240ml/1 cup/ 8fl.oz milk

+/- salt and pepper to taste

1 tsp dried dill

1. Whisk the eggs with a fork.

2. Whisk in the milk, salt, pepper and dill.

3. Add the diced salmon and cream cheese.

4. Mix gently with the fork.

5. Pour into a greased lined dish. Move the pieces of salmon around until they are evenly distributed.

6. Bake at 180C/350F for 30 minutes.

Serving size: 1 Serve (serves 10) | Calories: 207 | Fat: 16.2g | Total carbs: 2.2g
Sugar: 1.7g | Protein: 17.2g

Caesar salad

Caesar salad
quick, healthy and balanced

LCHF Caesar salad is the ultimate LCHF meal. It is incredibly low in carbs, and has moderate protein and plenty of healthy fats. It is whole food, it is unprocessed and it is nutritious. You can add whatever you have in the fridge.

Large handful of leafy greens – such as baby kale

Sliced spring onions

4 baby tomatoes, halved

Cucumber cubes

Cooked chicken

Blue cheese

Parmesan

Homemade mayonnaise

Anchovies

1. Layer the leafy greens and salad ingredients on the bottom of the serving dish.
2. Place the chicken and cheeses on top.
3. Pop the anchovies on to finish it off.
4. Drizzle with homemade mayonnaise.

There is no nutrition guide because the salad varies each time you make it.

Courgette &
feta fritters

Courgette & feta fritters
only four ingredients

When courgettes/zucchini are in season, buy up large and make huge batches of these courgette, mint and feta fritters. They are so delicious, colourful and nutritious. Keep the extra for lunch the next day at work or school. Many fritters have wheat, flour or other agents to bind them together. You don't need any of these – just four ingredients go into these low-carb fritters.

4 or 5 courgettes/zucchini, grated

50g / ½ cup feta, cut into cubes

Handful of fresh mint, roughly chopped

2 eggs

Coconut oil or butter for frying

1. Grate/shred the courgette/zucchini and squeeze out all the excess water.

2. Add the mint, feta and eggs and stir through.

3. Heat a frying pan and add fry small batches in coconut oil or butter until golden.

TOP TIP: If your courgette/zucchini fritters have always turned out soggy, it will be because you haven't squeezed out enough water as you are grating/shredding the courgette/zucchini. Also don't add salt to the mixture as that draws out even more water, have salt at the dinner table and season them then. Stir the mixture each time before you add another spoon to the frying pan, the egg has a tendency to drain to the bottom.

Serving size: 1 Serve (serves 10) | Calories: 207 | Fat: 16.2g | Total carbs: 2.2g
Sugar: 1.7g | Fibre: 2.6g | Protein: 9.8g

Salmon zoodles

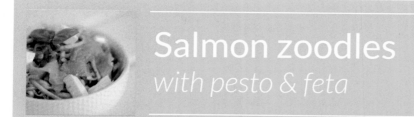

Salmon zoodles
with pesto & feta

Salmon zoodles with pesto and feta is an incredibly simple 'throw it all together' kinda meal. Simply put, zoodles are the low carb equivalent of noodles, only made with zucchini/ courgettes. They can be eaten raw or steamed to gently warm them through.

8 medium courgettes/zucchini – will make approx 8 cups zoodles

100g/3.5 oz smoked salmon pieces (alternatively, you can use freshly cooked salmon)

50g/2 oz/⅓ cup kale pesto

50g/2 oz/⅓ cup feta, cut into cubes

Lemon juice – optional

Amounts of all ingredients are approximate and can be adjusted to taste

1. Prepare the courgettes/zucchini by using your spiraliser. Steam gently if you would like a warm salmon zoodle salad.

2. Gently stir through the kale pesto, feta and salmon.

3. Serve in individual bowls and squeeze some lemon juice over each bowl (optional).

Serving size: 1 Serve (serves 4) | Calories: 175 | Fat: 12.5g | Total carbs: 8.6g
Sugar: 6g | Fibre: 2.6g | Protein: 9.8g

notes

– Low Carb –
Dinner

- Leafy lasagne
- Spaghetti bolognese & zoodles
- Bacon-covered meatloaf
- Self-saucing meatballs – in the slow cooker
- Slow-cooker beef stroganoff

Leafy lasagne

Leafy lasagne
with a cheat's cheese sauce

Leafy lasagne ends up with the most amazing layers of greens, meat and my special cheat's cheese sauce. Serve with a colourful leafy green salad and olive oil. Slices well for lunch the next day.

Meat layer
Oil for frying

1 onion, finely diced

1 kg/2 lb mince/ground beef

½ cup vegetable stock

2 tbsp tomato paste

400g/13 oz canned tomatoes

1 tbsp of dried rosemary, oregano and sage (or 3 tbsp mixed herbs)

Cheat's cheese sauce
300 ml/1 ¼ cup natural unsweetened yoghurt

3 egg yolks

200g/3 cups shredded/grated cheese

Salt/pepper to taste

100g/3 cups spinach leaves

Meat layer
1. Gently fry the onion in oil until clear but not browned.

2. Add the mince/ground beef and stir until all the meat is browned and cooked.

3. Add the vegetable stock, tomato paste, canned tomatoes and herbs.

4. Cook on a low medium heat for 10 minutes while you make the cheat's cheese sauce.

Cheats Cheese Sauce
1. Mix all the ingredients together

Putting it all together
1. Place half the meat on the bottom of a large baking/lasagne dish.

2. Place half the spinach leaves over the top of the meat.

3. Place half the cheat's cheese sauce over the spinach.

4. Repeat steps 1, 2, 3. Cover with another layer of grated/shredded cheese if you like.

5. Bake at 180C/350F for 20 minutes until golden brown.

Serving size: 1 serving (serves 8) | Calories: 452 | Fat: 28g | Total carbs: 7.6g
Sugar: 4.1g | Fibre: 2g | Protein: 42g

Spaghetti bolognese
& zoodles

Spaghetti bolognese & zoodles
a family favourite

Spaghetti bolognese is an absolute staple in our house. It can be ready in 20 minutes, start to finish, and we always seem to have mince/ground beef in the fridge. Kids love this one.

1 onion, finely chopped

2 cloves garlic, crushed

500g/1 lb mince/ground beef

400g/14 oz tinned or fresh, chopped tomatoes

Selection of fresh or dried Italian herbs - I use the following
1 tbs dried rosemary
1 tbs dried oregano
1 tbs dried sage
1 tbs dried basil
1 tbs dried marjoram

+/- Salt and pepper to taste

Zucchini/courgettes for zoodles

Parmesan

1. In a large saucepan. gently fry the onion and garlic in oil until softened but not overcooked.

2. Add the mince/ground beef and continue to cook whilst stirring continuously to break up the mince/ground beef. Cook until all the meat is browned.

3. Add the herbs, seasoning and tomatoes.

4. Stir, then simmer for 15 minutes while you make the zoodles.

5. To make zoodles, wash and trim the ends of your zucchini. Turn the zucchini in a spiraliser or a handheld shredder to create the pasta/noodle shape. Zoodles can be lightly steamed for a few minutes. Drain well and allow excess steam to escape

6. Serve in a bowl with steamed zoodles and grated cheese or Parmesan sprinkled on top.

Nutrition Notes ::
Zoodles are an incredibly fresh and healthy alternative to pasta. Pasta 1 cup cooked = 221 calories, 43g carbs. Zucchini 1 cup = 25 calories, 4.6g carbs and additional vitamins, nutrients and antioxidants not found in processed pasta.

Serving size: 1 serve with zoodles | Calories: 318 | Fat: 17g | Total carbs: 13g
Sugar: 7g | Fibre: 4g | Protein: 30g

Bacon-covered meatloaf

Bacon-covered meatloaf
a fabulous way to hide vegetables

This is a superb way to hide some extra vegetables if you have reluctant children. It can be frozen and fabulous for school lunch boxes the next day.

1 spring onion, sliced

2 garlic cloves, crushed

750g/1.6 lb mince/ground beef

750g/1.6 lb mince/ground pork

2 eggs, lightly beaten

Handful fresh parsley, chopped

Handful fresh basil, chopped

2 slices bacon, diced

30g/1 oz chopped sun-dried tomatoes (optional)

2 tsp dried oregano

+/- Salt and pepper to taste

Grated vegetables of choice can also be added

Slices of bacon to cover the meatloaf

1. Oil and line a baking tray before starting.

2. Put all the ingredients in a large mixing bowl and mix together with your hands until all the ingredients are thoroughly incorporated together.

3. Form into a large meatloaf shape on the lined baking tray. Cover with the bacon slices and sprinkle on Parmesan cheese (optional).

4. Bake at 180C/350F for 50 minutes or until thoroughly cooked in the centre.

Serving size: 1 Slice (serves 12) | Calories: 370 | Fat: 25g | Total carbs: 1.2g
Sugar: 0.6g | Fibre: 0.2g | Protein: 35g

Self-saucing
meatballs

Self-saucing meatballs
in the slow cooker

Learn to love your slow cooker. You can prepare it in the morning, or even prepare the night before, then in the morning pop it inside the slow cooker and turn it on.

Meatballs

1 onion, quartered

2 whole garlic cloves, crushed

2 slices bacon, diced

1 kg/2.2 lb ground/mince beef

Favourite herbs – I use rosemary, thyme, marjoram and sage

1 egg

+/- Salt and pepper to taste

Self-saucing tomato sauce
2 x 400g/14 oz chopped tinned/canned tomatoes

Meatballs
1. Oil the inside of the slow cooker dish so the meatballs won't stick.

2. Place the quartered onions, whole garlic and bacon in the food processor. Pulse until finely chopped.

3. Add the ground/mince meat, herbs and egg. Pulse until smooth.

4. Remove the blade and roll a generous spoon of the mixture into meatballs, placing each one into the slow cooker dish.

Self-saucing tomato sauce
1. Pour the tinned chopped tomatoes over the meatballs. You can use fresh tomatoes but the tinned tomatoes tend to work better and produce a thick sauce.

2. I cook on LOW for 6–10 hours or HIGH for 4–6 hours. But be guided by your own experience with your own slow cooker instructions as they all vary.

Serving size: 1 serve meatballs and sauce | Calories: 358 | Fat: 22g | Total carbs: 5.2g
Sugar: 2.8g | Fibre: 1g | Protein: 33.9g

Slow-cooker
beef stroganoff

Slow-cooker beef stroganoff
incredibly delicious

How wonderful to come home after a long and busy day to a home-cooked meal. Garnish with sour cream and serve with steamed vegetables and butter.

1 brown onion, sliced and quartered

2 cloves garlic, crushed

2 slices streaky bacon, diced

500g/1.1 lb beef stewing steak, cubed

1 tsp smoked paprika

¼ cup tomato paste

250ml (1 cup) beef stock

250g/9 oz mushrooms, quartered

1. Place all the ingredients in the slow cooker.
2. Mix.
3. Set on LOW for 6–8 hours or HIGH 4–6 hours.
4. Serve with sour cream/cream cheese.

Serving size: 1 Serve (serves 6) | Calories: 260 | Fat: 14.2g | Total carbs: 6g
Sugar: 3.2g | Fibre: 1.2g | Protein: 26.5g

notes

– Low Carb –
Snacks

- Parmesan crisps
- Sugar-free granola bars
- Cracker crackling
- Cream cheese stuffed meatballs
- FatHead crackers

Parmesan crisps

Parmesan crisps
super simple

There are only two ingredients here – Parmesan and herbs. You can easily turn that shredded/ grated Parmesan into a crisp that is crunchy and cheesey. Perfect for a snack, for floating on soup, or use as crunchy croutons for a Caesar salad.

1 cup /100g grated/shredded Parmesan cheese

Herbs or spices such as garlic, chilli, rosemary, cracked pepper to taste

1. Mix the shredded/grated Parmesan with the herbs or spices.

2. Place small rounds on a parchment lined baking sheet. I use a circle cookie cutter to get a perfect round shape. Allow enough room for each Parmesan crisp to melt and spread while cooking.

3. Alternatively, you can spread the entire mixture in one layer and bake until crisp, then snap into pieces or use a pizza cutting wheel to slice into squares.

4. Bake at 180C/350F for 4–8 minutes until golden.

5. Remove from the oven and allow to cool on the lined baking sheet, or remove and place over an upside down oiled muffin tin to create Parmesan 'cups'.

Serving size: 1per Parmesan crisp (makes 16) | Calories: 26 | Fat: 1.7g | Total carbs: 0.8g
Sugar: 0g | Fibre: 0g | Protein: 1.8g

Sugar-free
granola bars

Sugar-free granola bars
great for school lunches

Store-bought granola/muesli bars appear to be healthy but contain an astounding amount of sugar. Avoid bars which contain dried fruit – they're sugar dense and have very little nutrition. These can be made nut free for those with allergies.

350g/12 oz mixed nuts and/or seeds

50g/1.8 oz shredded coconut

2 tbsp cocoa nibs

50g/1.8 oz coconut oil

4 tbsp tahini or nut butter

1 tsp vanilla

2 tsp dried cinnamon
pinch salt

3 tbsp granulated sweetener of choice, to taste

2 eggs

1. Place all the ingredients in the blender.

2. Pulse a few times until combined and still pieces of nuts and seeds can be seen.

3. Place in a greased and lined 18cmx27cm/7x10 inch baking dish. If you bake it in a large dish, it will turn thin and crispy which can also be really nice.

4. Bake at 180C/350F for 20 minutes or until golden, not burnt.

5. Can be drizzled with 90% chocolate.

Serving size: 1 bar | Calories: 234 | Fat: 20.5g | Total carbs: 6.9g
Sugar: 0.9g | Fibre: 4.5g | Protein: 7g

Cracker
crackling

Cracker crackling
crispy pork rinds

I love crackling, but I find the crackling you buy in stores is expensive, packed in artificial flavourings and preservatives, and generally cooked in canola (rapeseed) oil. My secret method also uses no knives – so no cut fingers.

Sheets of pork crackling

Oil

Salt

+/- Herbs or spices

1. Place the pork crackling on an oiled baking tray with a lip/side/edge. Season with salt and/or herbs and spices.

2. Cook at 180C/350F for 10 minutes until soft.

3. Remove from the oven and using kitchen tongs and kitchen scissors, cut into strips or shapes.

4. Cook until golden and crispy. Turn once or twice during cooking.

5. Drain the crackling and pour the rendered pork fat into a heatproof jug.

6. Cool the rendered fat and use as cooking lard. Store the lard in the fridge.

Serving size: Per 100g | Calories: 544 | Fat: 31g | Total carbs: 0g | Protein: 61g

Cream cheese
stuffed meatballs

Cream cheese stuffed meatballs
can be frozen

These are what dreams are made of. They are quick to make, economical, perfect as a snack, lunch, dinner, breakfast (you know I think leftovers are King!) and can be frozen. So why not make a double, triple batch and be prepared for the weeks ahead?

Meatballs

1 spring onion, finely sliced

1 garlic clove, crushed

750g/1.6 lb ground/mince meat of choice (I used pork)

+/- Salt and pepper to taste

1 egg, slightly beaten

2 slices bacon, finely chopped

3 tbsp sundried tomatoes, finely diced

2 tbsp of your favourite herbs – I use rosemary, thyme, oregano and sage

Filling

100g/3.5 oz cream cheese, diced into squares

Meatballs
1. Place all the meatball ingredients on a large mixing bowl. Mix thoroughly with your hands.

2. Using a dessert spoon, scoop up a golf-ball size of meatball mixture.

3. Squeeze the mixture into a ball then flatten into a disc.

Filling
1. Place a cube of cream cheese in the centre of the meatball circle then enclose the meatball mixture around the cream cheese. Place the cream cheese stuffed meatball on a greased baking tray.

2. Repeat until all the mixture has been used. Spray them all with olive oil spray so they will crisp and brown beautifully.

3. Bake at 180C/350F for 15–20 minutes depending on your oven, or until golden brown.

Serving size: 1 Meatball | Calories: 103 | Fat: 7.5g | Total carbs: 0.7g
Sugar: 0.4g | Fibre: 0.08g | Protein: 7.8g

FatHead
crackers

FatHead crackers
cheesy heaven

The Holy Grail of low-carb pizza has now become a cracker – FatHead crackers. Grain-free, crisp, cheesy heaven. FatHead pizza is the most downloaded recipe for the entire site.

170g/6 oz/1¾ cups (approx) shredded/grated cheese (mozzarella is the best or Edam/ mild cheese)

2 tbsp cream cheese

1 egg

85g/3 oz/½ cup almond flour/meal

+/- Salt to taste

½ tsp flavourings of choice (optional)

1. Put the shredded/grated cheese and cream cheese in a microwaveable bowl. Microwave on HIGH for 1 minute.

2. Stir then microwave on HIGH for another 30 seconds.

3. Add the egg, salt, flavourings and ground almonds, mix gently.

4. Place in between 2 pieces of baking parchment and roll thinly. Remove top parchement. If the mixture hardens and becomes difficult to work with, pop it back in the microwave for 10–20 seconds to soften again but not too long or you will cook the egg.

5. Cut the dough using a pizza cutter or sharp knife into small cracker shapes. Place each one on a lined baking tray as shown.

6. Bake at 220C/425F for 5 minutes on each side, or until browned on both side and crisp.

7. Cool on a wire rack and keep in an airtight container in the fridge. If the weather is cool, you may store the container on your pantry for up to 3 days.

Serving size: 1 Serve (serves 6) | Calories: 260 | Fat: 14.2g | Total carbs: 6g
Sugar: 3.2g | Fibre: 1.2g | Protein: 26.5g

notes

– Low Carb –
Sweets

- Chocolate zucchini cake
- Boozy brandy truffles
- Orange & almond flourless cake
- Flourless berry sponge
- NY baked cheesecake

Chocolate
zucchini cake

Chocolate zucchini cake
a sneaky way to eat your greens

This exclusive recipe is a wonderful alternative to a heavy chocolate cake and another way to get some more vegetables into your reluctant children. It is an incredibly moist and soft cake.

Chocolate zucchini cake

220g/8 oz/1 cup butter, softened

3-5 tbsp granulated sweetener of choice, to taste

2 tsp vanilla essence or paste

5 medium eggs

200g/7 oz/2 cup almond flour/ meal

2 tsp baking powder

45g/1.5 oz/½ cup unsweetened cocoa powder

4 cups grated/shredded zucchini/ courgettes, loosely packed. After you have measured the 4 cups, squeeze out some of the liquid so the cake isn't soggy

Optional
Whipped cream and strawberries to decorate

Chocolate zucchini cake
1. Place the softened butter, stevia, vanilla in a mixing bowl and mix until smooth.

2. Add the eggs one by one, mixing in between each egg.

3. Add the almond flour/meal, baking powder, and cocoa. Mix until smooth.

4. Stir in the grated/shredded zucchini/courgette and mix gently until the zucchini is hidden in the chocolate cake mixture.

5. Divide the mixture between 2 sandwich baking tins which have been oiled and lined.

6. Bake at 180C/350F for 25–30 minutes until completely cooked in the centre but still remains moist.

To Decorate
1. Whip some double/heavy/whipping cream and use it to sandwich the 2 cake layers together.

2. Place more whipped cream on top of the double layer cake and decorate with sliced strawberries, or berries of choice.

Serving size: 1 double layer iced slice (seves 10) | Calories: 407 | Fat: 39g | Total carbs: 9.6g
Sugar: 3.2g | Fibre: 4.4g | Protein: 9.5g

Boozy brandy
truffles

Boozy brandy truffles
one for the adults

These are intended for adults only as they contain alcohol. If you would like these to be alcohol free, you can omit the brandy entirely, or use alcohol-free brandy essence.

250g/9 oz regular cream cheese block (not spreadable)

100g/3.5 oz butter, melted

4 tbsp unsweetened dark cocoa powder

¼ cup walnut pieces

3 tbsp granulated sweetener of choice, to taste

1–2 tbsp brandy (see note above)

1. Warm the cream cheese block to room temperature or in the microwave for 15 seconds, until it is soft enough to work with.

2. Add the melted butter and mix through with a fork to ensure it is lump free and smooth.

3. Add the cocoa powder, stevia and brandy. Mix until thoroughly combined.

4. Gently stir through the tiny walnut pieces and refrigerate until firm enough to roll into balls.

5. Roll a heaped teaspoon at a time and place each truffle on a plate. Place the plate into the fridge again for an hour or two for the truffles to really set firmly.

6. Roll in cocoa powder if you like, or crushed walnuts, pistachios, pecans etc.

Serving size: 1 truffle | Calories: 94 | Fat: 9.6g | Total carbs: 1.3g
Sugar: 0.5g | Fibre: 0.5g | Protein: 1.4g

Orange & almond
flourless cake

Orange & almond flourless cake
a simple blender cake

This recipe use a whole orange – skin and all – so only one fruit is required to get that delicious citrus taste. You simply add all the ingredients and pulse until smooth in the blender.

Orange and almond flourless cake

1 orange, quartered

6 eggs

250g/9 oz almond flour/meal

1 tsp baking powder

3 - 4 tbsp granulated sweetener of choice, to taste

1 tsp vanilla

¼ tsp salt

Sugar-free icing

100g/3.5 oz unsweetened natural yoghurt

100g/3.5 oz softened cream cheese

50g/1.8 oz sugar-free confectioners/icing powder

2 tbsp orange zest to taste

Orange and almond flourless cake

1. Remove any seeds and place the orange quarters in the food processor. Using the blade attachment, blitz until almost pureed. It is nice to see small pieces of orange peel in the final baking mix.

2. Add all the other ingredients. Pulse until smooth.

3. Pour into 2 greased and lined sponge tins.

4. Bake at 180C/350F for 20–25 minutes. Test the centre with a clean fork or skewer to ensure it is cooked thoroughly.

Sugar-free icing

1. Mix the softened cream cheese with the natural yoghurt with a fork until smooth.

2. Add the orange zest and sugar-free confectioners/icing powder.

3. When the cakes are completely cold, place the first layer on the serving plate and ice with the sugar-free confectioners/icing powder. Place the other cake layer on top and sprinkle with the sugar free sugar-free confectioners/icing powder and tiny pieces of orange zest and orange slices.

Serving size: 1 iced double layer slice | Calories: 197 | Fat: 16g | Total carbs: 7.9g
Sugar: 3.1g | Fibre: 3g | Protein: 8.3g

Flourless
berry sponge

Flourless berry sponge
light and delicate

Coconut flour is lovely to use in low-carb cakes. It is incredibly absorbent so you only use a small amount. Add plenty of vanilla and butter to make it creamy yet light.

110g/4 oz/1 stick butter melted

½ cup coconut flour

3 –5 tbsp granulated sweetener of choice, to taste

2 tsp vanilla

1 tsp baking powder

8 eggs

1 cup frozen berries

1. Mix the melted butter, coconut flour, stevia, vanilla and baking powder together until smooth.

2. Add the eggs one by one, mixing in between each addition.

3. Pour into a prepared baking dish – I use a silicon cake dish.

4. Press each frozen berry evenly into the cake. This allows the berries to be evenly distributed and not clump together. It also stops the cake from turning pink!

5. Bake at 180C/350F for 20–25 minutes until cooked in the centre.

6. Serve with yoghurt and berries.

TOP TIP: When I add frozen berries to a cake, I wait until the mixture is in the baking dish, then press the frozen berries in the batter so they are evenly distributed and don't colour the cake batter.

Serving size: 1 slice (serves 10) | Calories: 176 | Fat: 13.8g | Total carbs: 7.2g
Sugar: : 2.3g | Fibre: 3.6g | Protein: 5.6g

NY baked
cheesecake

NY baked cheesecake
with an easy chocolate ganache

If you love a simple baked cheesecake then this is for you. If you don't like cinnamon, you can use vanilla instead

Base

3 tbsp granulated sweetener of choice, to taste

110g/½ cup/1 stick butter, softened

1 tsp vanilla

1 egg

100g/3.5 oz/1 cup almond meal/flour

½ cup coconut flour

1 tsp salt

1 tsp ground cinnamon

Cheesecake filling

300g/10.5 oz/1⅓ cup full-fat cream cheese (not spreadable)

1 tsp cinnamon

2 eggs

Chocolate ganache

250ml 1 cup double/heavy cream

300g/10 oz dark 85% chocolate, broken into pieces

Base
1. Prepare the baking dish by rubbing butter on the bottom and sides, then lining the base with baking paper.

2. Mix all the ingredients together until it is the consistency of peanut butter. Smooth the mixture into the prepared dish.

3. Bake at 180C/350 F for 10 minutes until golden.

Cheesecake filling
1. Put the cream cheese, eggs and cinnamon into a bowl and blend with a stick blender/immersion blender until completely smooth.

2. Pour onto the baked base, then return to the oven and bake at 180C/350F for another 20 minutes.

3. Allow to cool before refrigerating.

Chocolate ganache
1. Place the cream into a saucepan and gently heat until warm but NOT boiling.

2. Remove from heat, add the chcolate pieces and mix. Continue to stir until thick and glossy.

3. Pour over the cold cheesecake and refrigerate until set.

Serving size: 1 slice, serves 12 | Calories: 479 | Fat: 39g | Total carbs: 15.3g
Sugar: 5.3g | Fibre: 6.3g | Protein: 9.5g

Don't compare
your journey
to anyone else's

WEEKLY MEAL PLAN & SHOPPING LIST

MEASUREMENT TRACKER

Weekly Meal Plan

Date: June 20   to: June 26

:: Monday ::

B — Boiled eggs and cheese soldiers

L — Salmon zoodles

D — Lasagne

:: Tuesday ::

B — Grain-free granola with unsweetened yoghurt

L — Caesar salad

D — Meatloaf

:: Wednesday ::

B — Smoked salmon scrambled eggs

L — Meatloaf

D — Salmon quiche

:: Thursday ::

B — Grain-free granola with unsweetened yoghurt

L — Salmon Quiche

D — Meatballs

:: Friday ::

B — Boiled eggs and cheese soldiers

L — Courgette fritters

D — Spaghetti bolognese

:: Saturday ::

B — Keto waffles with cream and berries

L — Skillet bread

D — Stroganoff

:: Sunday ::

B — Breakfast McMuggins

L — Skillet bread

D — Salmon quiche

Shopping list

ground/mince beef	feta
smoked salmon	butter
casserole beef	variety of cheeses
gound/mince pork	eggs
bacon	cream cheese (full-fat)
salmon fillet/tin/can	unweeetened yoghurt
cooked chicken	cream
spinach	coconut oil
kale	extra virgin olive oil
zucchini	
spring onion	canned/tinned tomatoes
leafy greens	tomato paste
fresh mint	herbs, spices
onion	vanilla, anchovies
mushrooms	frozen berries,
almond flour/meal	cacao nibs
coconut flour	unsweetened shredded coconut
variety of seeds and nuts	psyllium husk
sweetener of choice	

Note :: Many of these may be in your pantry already.

B *Breakfast*   L *Lunch*   D *Dinner*

www.ditchthecarbs.com

Weekly Meal Plan

Date: _____ to: _____

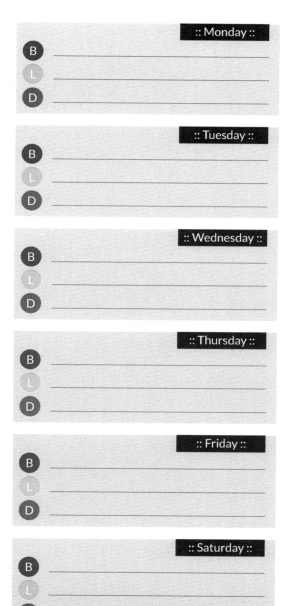

:: Monday ::
B _____
L _____
D _____

:: Tuesday ::
B _____
L _____
D _____

:: Wednesday ::
B _____
L _____
D _____

:: Thursday ::
B _____
L _____
D _____

:: Friday ::
B _____
L _____
D _____

:: Saturday ::
B _____
L _____
D _____

:: Sunday ::
B _____
L _____
D _____

Shopping list

 Breakfast   *Lunch* D *Dinner*

This page is free to copy and use

www.ditchthecarbs.com

DITCH *the* CARBS

Weekly Meal Plan

Date: _____ to: _____

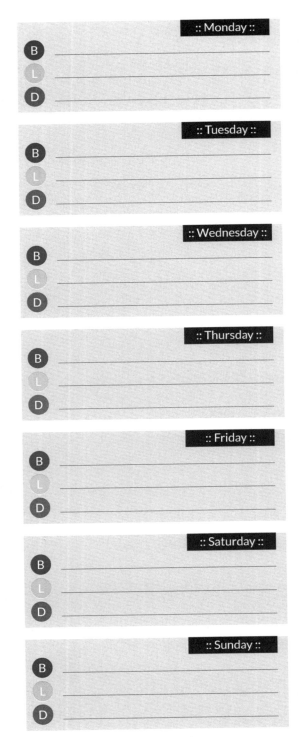

Shopping list

 Breakfast   Lunch   Dinner

This page is free to copy and use

www.ditchthecarbs.com

Weekly Meal Plan

Date: _____ to: _____

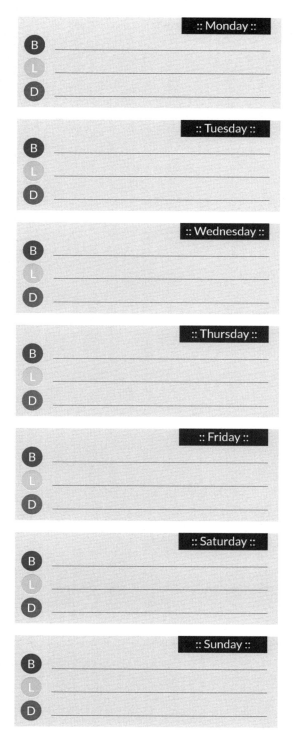

:: Monday ::
- B _____
- L _____
- D _____

:: Tuesday ::
- B _____
- L _____
- D _____

:: Wednesday ::
- B _____
- L _____
- D _____

:: Thursday ::
- B _____
- L _____
- D _____

:: Friday ::
- B _____
- L _____
- D _____

:: Saturday ::
- B _____
- L _____
- D _____

:: Sunday ::
- B _____
- L _____
- D _____

Shopping list

B *Breakfast*   **L** *Lunch*   **D** *Dinner*

This page is free to copy and use

www.ditchthecarbs.com

DITCH the CARBS

MEASUREMENT TRACKERS

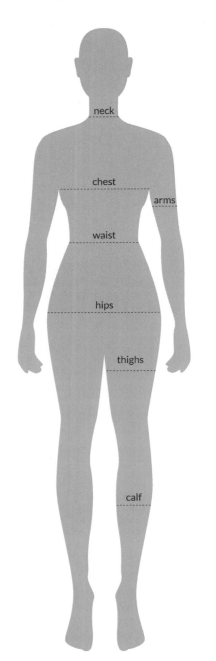

neck

chest

arms

waist

hips

thighs

calf

MEASUREMENT PROGRESS

Date	June 3	June 10	June 17					
Neck	18.5	18.5	18.25					
Chest	37	36.5	36.5					
Waist	32	32	31.5					
Hips	42	41.5	41.25					
Arms	13	13.2	13					
Thighs	22	21	20.5					
Calf	16	16	16					

WEIGHT LOSS/GAIN PROGRESS

WAIST LOSS/GAIN PROGRESS

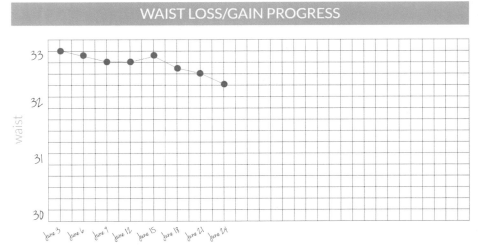

MEASUREMENT TRACKERS

MEASUREMENT PROGRESS

Date								
Neck								
Chest								
Waist								
Hips								
Arms								
Thighs								
Calf								

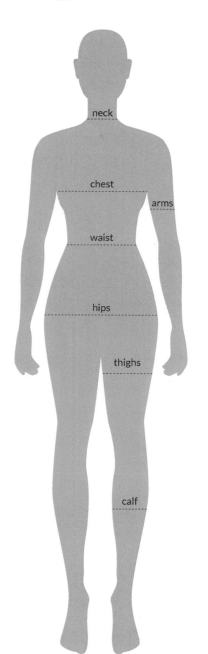

WEIGHT LOSS/GAIN PROGRESS

weight

WAIST LOSS/GAIN PROGRESS

waist

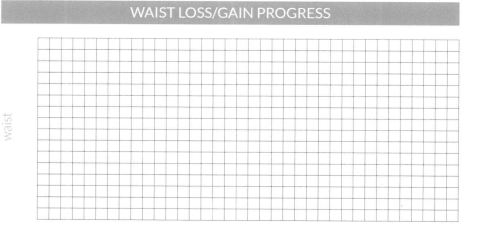

This page is free to copy and use

MEASUREMENT TRACKERS

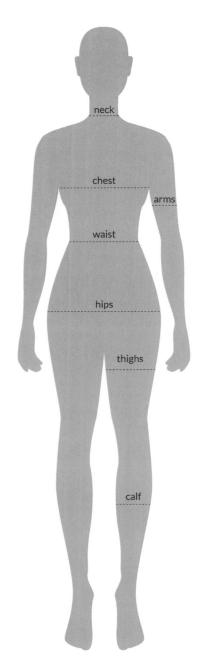

MEASUREMENT PROGRESS

Date								
Neck								
Chest								
Waist								
Hips								
Arms								
Thighs								
Calf								

WEIGHT LOSS/GAIN PROGRESS

weight

WAIST LOSS/GAIN PROGRESS

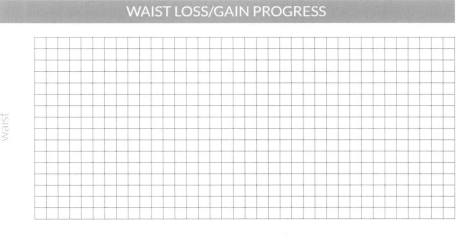

waist

This page is free to copy and use

MEASUREMENT TRACKERS

MEASUREMENT PROGRESS

Date								
Neck								
Chest								
Waist								
Hips								
Arms								
Thighs								
Calf								

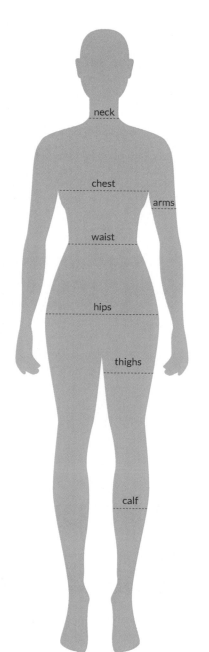

WEIGHT LOSS/GAIN PROGRESS

weight

WAIST LOSS/GAIN PROGRESS

waist

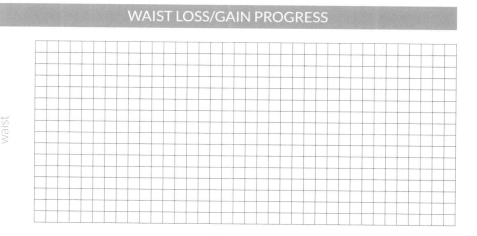

This page is free to copy and use

Be proud
of any changes
you have made

Made in the USA
Middletown, DE
27 January 2018